SADDLE UP!

Arabian Horses

by Rachel Grack

BLASTOFF!
2
READERS

BELLWETHER MEDIA • MINNEAPOLIS, MN

Blastoff! Readers are carefully developed by literacy experts to build reading stamina and move students toward fluency by combining standards-based content with developmentally appropriate text.

Level 1 provides the most support through repetition of high-frequency words, light text, predictable sentence patterns, and strong visual support.

Level 2 offers early readers a bit more challenge through varied sentences, increased text load, and text-supportive special features.

Level 3 advances early-fluent readers toward fluency through increased text load, less reliance on photos, advancing concepts, longer sentences, and more complex special features.

★ **Blastoff! Universe**

Reading Level

Grade
K

Grades
1–3

Grade
4

This edition first published in 2021 by Bellwether Media, Inc.

No part of this publication may be reproduced in whole or in part without written permission of the publisher. For information regarding permission, write to Bellwether Media, Inc., Attention: Permissions Department, 6012 Blue Circle Drive, Minnetonka, MN 55343.

Library of Congress Cataloging-in-Publication Data

Names: Koestler-Grack, Rachel A., 1973- author.
Title: Arabian horses / by Rachel Grack.
Description: Minneapolis, MN : Bellwether Media, Inc., 2021. | Series: Blastoff! readers: saddle up! | Includes bibliographical references and index. | Audience: Ages 5-8 | Audience: Grades K-1 | Summary: "Relevant images match informative text in this introduction to Arabian horses. Intended for students in kindergarten through third grade"–Provided by publisher
Identifiers: LCCN 2019054277 (print) | LCCN 2019054278 (ebook) | ISBN 9781644872345 (library binding) | ISBN 9781618919922 (ebook)
Subjects: LCSH: Arabian horse–Juvenile literature.
Classification: LCC SF293.A8 K64 2021 (print) | LCC SF293.A8 (ebook) | DDC 636.1/12–dc23
LC record available at https://lccn.loc.gov/2019054277
LC ebook record available at https://lccn.loc.gov/2019054278

Editor: Elizabeth Neuenfeldt   Designer: Andrea Schneider

Printed in the United States of America, North Mankato, MN.

Table of Contents

Fast Travelers

Arabian horses live all around the world.

They are quick and strong. Some can run up to 40 miles (65 kilometers) per hour!

Outstanding Beauty

dished face

Arabian horses stand out! They have **dished** faces and large, dark eyes.

These horses also have a bump on their foreheads. It is called a **jibbah**.

jibbah

Arabian horses stand between 14 and 15 **hands** high.

They have curved necks and strong bodies. They also have short backs and high **tail carriages**.

tail carriage

SIZE OF AN ARABIAN HORSE

20 hands

14 to 15 hands

12 hands

10 hands

0 hands

one hand = 4 inches (10 centimeters)

9

Arabian horses have soft **coats** and **manes**. Many are **chestnut**, gray, or black.

chestnut

gray

black

mane

They often have white markings on their faces or legs.

Arabian Horse Beginnings

Arabian horses in the Middle East

Arabian horses are one of the oldest horse **breeds**.

They came from the **Middle East** as early as 1500 BCE! They are named for the Arabian **Peninsula**.

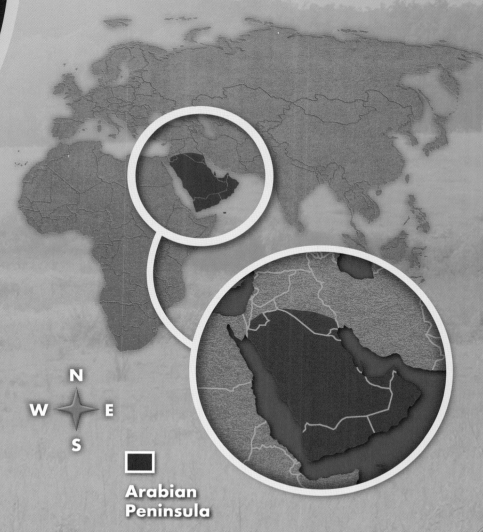

N
W E
S

Arabian Peninsula

In 1877, the **sultan** of Turkey sent two Arabian horses to America. Many people liked them!

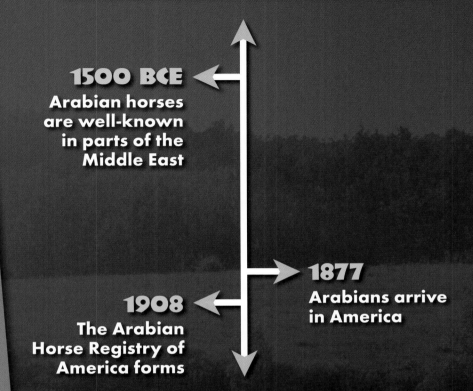

ARABIAN HORSE TIMELINE

1500 BCE
Arabian horses are well-known in parts of the Middle East

1877
Arabians arrive in America

1908
The Arabian Horse Registry of America forms

Soon, more arrived. The Arabian Horse Registry of America formed in 1908.

Strong and Smart

Arabian horses have great **endurance**.

They can run far on hard trails. Long ago, races across the desert lasted three days!

jumping

Arabians are smart and
easy to train. They make
excellent show horses.

Riders use them for **dressage** and jumping. These horses even have their own **trot**!

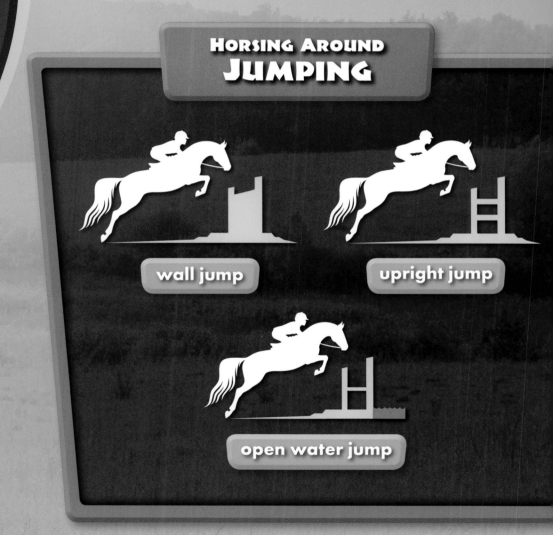

HORSING AROUND
JUMPING

wall jump

upright jump

open water jump

Arabians make good
horses for new riders, too.
They are kind and trusting.

These horses are great friends for everyone!

Glossary

breeds—certain types of horses

chestnut—a reddish-brown color

coats—the hair or fur covering some animals

dished—curved in

dressage—a horse show event judged on movement, balance, and the ability to follow directions

endurance—the ability to keep going for a long time

hands—the units used to measure the height of a horse; one hand is equal to 4 inches (10 centimeters).

jibbah—a shield-shaped bump on a horse's forehead

manes—hair that grows from the necks of horses

Middle East—parts of southwest Asia and northern Africa; the Middle East includes Egypt, Israel, Iran, Iraq, Lebanon, Saudi Arabia, Syria, and other nearby countries.

peninsula—a section of land that sticks out from a larger piece of land and is almost completely surrounded by water

sultan—king

tail carriages—where tails sit on the back ends of horses

trot—a way horses move that is faster than walking but slower than running; when horses trot, a front leg moves at the same time as an opposite back leg.

To Learn More

AT THE LIBRARY

Hansen, Grace. *Arabian Horses*. Minneapolis, Minn.: Abdo Kids, 2020.

Meister, Cari. *Arabian Horses*. Mankato, Minn.: Amicus, 2019.

Noll, Elizabeth. *Arabian Horses*. Mankato, Minn.: Black Rabbit Books, 2019.

ON THE WEB

FACTSURFER

Factsurfer.com gives you a safe, fun way to find more information.

1. Go to www.factsurfer.com.

2. Enter "Arabian horses" into the search box and click 🔍.

3. Select your book cover to see a list of related content.

Index

The images in this book are reproduced through the courtesy of: mariait, front cover (horse); Vova Shevchuk, pp. 2, 3, 23 (horseshoes); Nature Picture Library/ Alamy, pp. 4 (inset), 16 (inset); Rolf Kopfle/ Alamy, pp. 4-5; ashkabe, pp. 6-7 (top); Arco Images GmbH/ Alamy, p. 7; Olga_i, pp. 8 (inset), 10 (chestnut); Andrzej Kubik, pp. 8-9; arthorse, p. 10 (gray); Rkpimages, p. 10 (black); Sari ONeal, p. 11; Benny Marty, pp. 12-13; Kerrick, pp. 14-15; Hans Christiansson, pp. 16-17; Voyagerix, pp. 18-19; Juniors Bildarchiv GmbH/ Alamy, pp. 20 (bottom), 20-21.